W9-CYT-149

BRIGHT
IDEA
BOOKS

FAMOUS
Ghosts

by Tammy Gagne

CAPSTONE PRESS
a capstone imprint

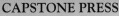

Bright Idea Books are published by Capstone Press
1710 Roe Crest Drive, North Mankato, Minnesota 56003
www.mycapstone.com

Library of Congress Cataloging-in-Publication Data
Names: Gagne, Tammy, author.
Title: Famous ghosts / by Tammy Gagne.
Description: North Mankato : Capstone Press, 2019. | Series: Ghosts and
   hauntings | Includes bibliographical references and index.
Identifiers: LCCN 2018018701 (print) | LCCN 2018020810 (ebook) | ISBN
   9781543541939 (ebook) | ISBN 9781543541533 (hardcover : alk. paper)
Subjects: LCSH: Ghosts--Juvenile literature. | Haunted places--Juvenile literature.
Classification: LCC BF1461 (ebook) | LCC BF1461 .G25 2019 (print) | DDC 133.1--dc23
LC record available at https://lccn.loc.gov/2018018701

Editorial Credits
Editor: Maddie Spalding
Designer: Becky Daum
Production Specialist: Colleen McLaren

Photo Credits
AP Images: Mark Humphrey, 15; iStockphoto: duncan1890, 5, EricVega, 31, Starcevic, 6–7, Yuri_Arcurs, cover (ghost); New York Public Library: Thomas Rowlandson/Jerome Robbins Dance Division, 22–23; Newscom: Jim West imageBROKER, 25; Shutterstock: Aleksei Isachenko, cover (blonde woman), Alena Gan, 8–9, Darla Hallmark, 18–19, ehrlif, 12–13, Eric Isselee, 11 (body), 28 (body), Haywiremedia, 11 (background), karenfoleyphotography, 26–27, Lepas, 11 (head), 28 (head), Paul Wishart, 21, prakashghai, cover (mirror), Underawesternsky, 17

Design Elements: iStockphoto, Red Line Editorial, and Shutterstock Images

TABLE OF CONTENTS

CHAPTER 1

BLOODY
Mary

Ghost stories have been around for a long time. Some are famous. The story of Bloody Mary is known around the world.

Queen Mary I of England was nicknamed "Bloody Mary."

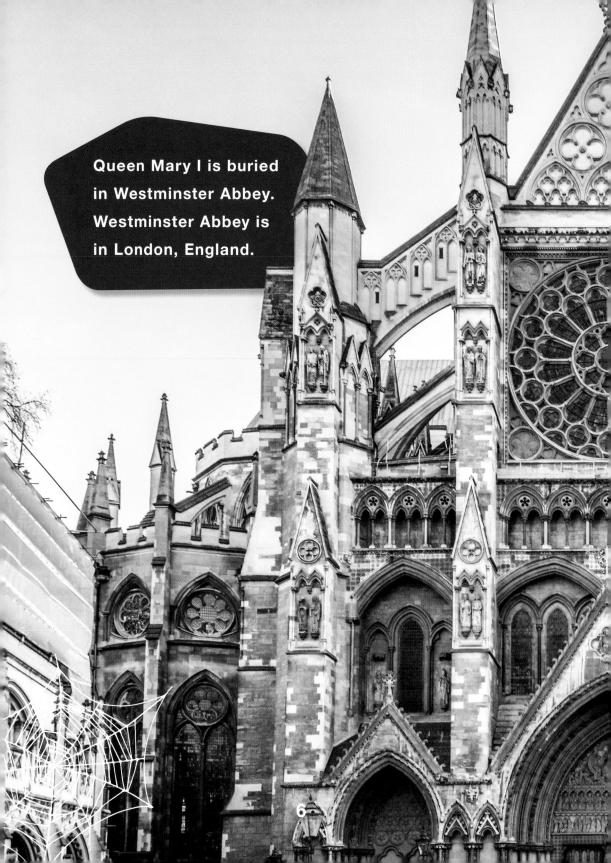

Queen Mary I is buried in Westminster Abbey. Westminster Abbey is in London, England.

6

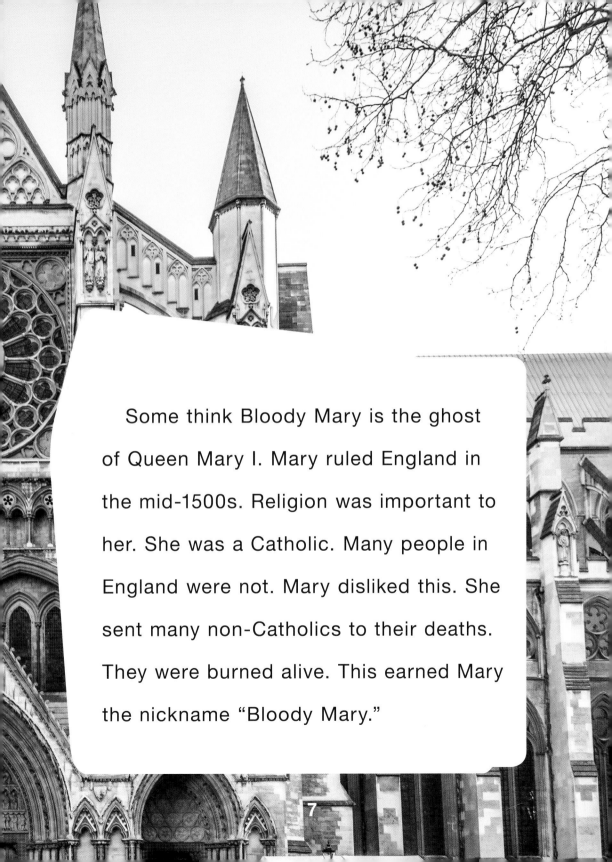

Some think Bloody Mary is the ghost of Queen Mary I. Mary ruled England in the mid-1500s. Religion was important to her. She was a Catholic. Many people in England were not. Mary disliked this. She sent many non-Catholics to their deaths. They were burned alive. This earned Mary the nickname "Bloody Mary."

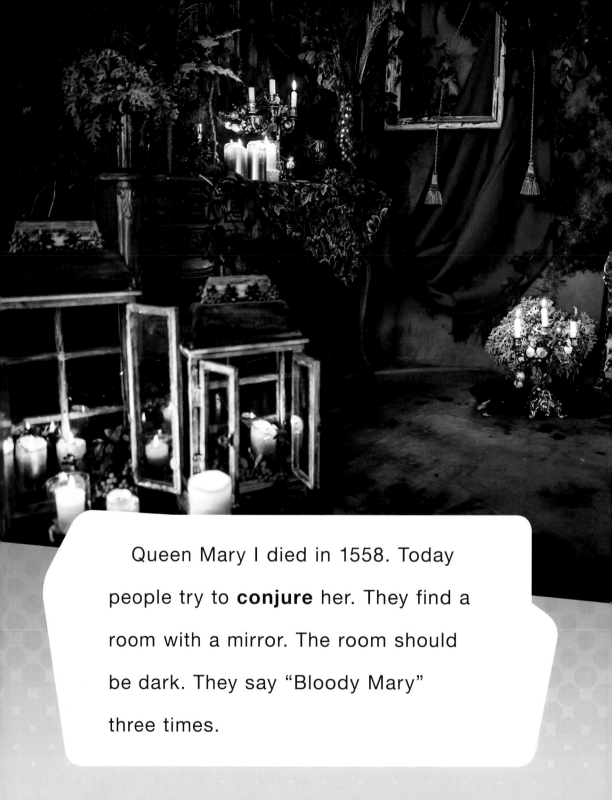

Queen Mary I died in 1558. Today people try to **conjure** her. They find a room with a mirror. The room should be dark. They say "Bloody Mary" three times.

Some people say you should light candles to conjure Bloody Mary.

They then wait for her ghost to appear. Some say the mirror will drip blood. Others say the ghost will reach out of the mirror. They say she will scratch your face!

CHAPTER 2

THE BELL WITCH
of Tennessee

In 1817 farmer John Bell saw a strange animal. It appeared near his house one night. It had a rabbit's head and a dog's body. Bell shot at it. But it disappeared. Stories say the creature was the ghost of a **witch**. They call it the Bell Witch.

The Bell Witch story has been told for more than 200 years.

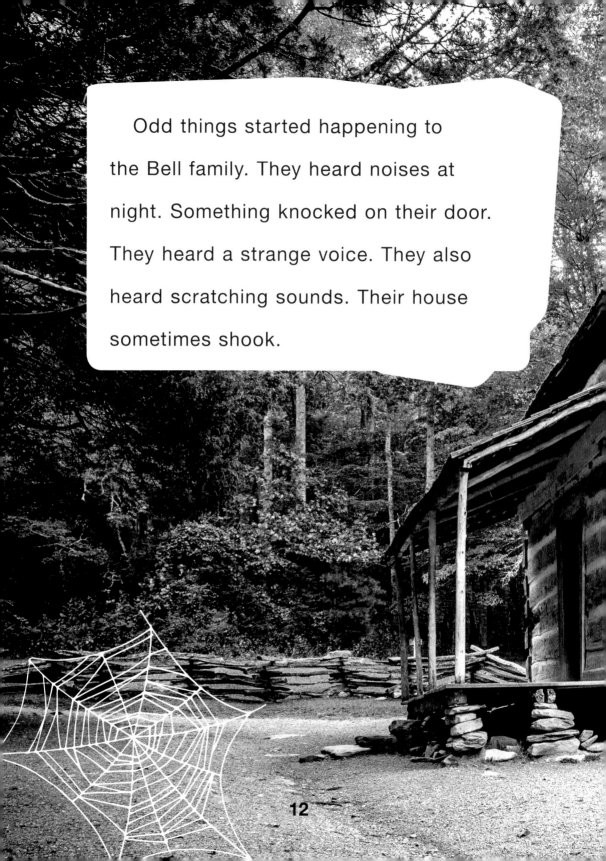

Odd things started happening to the Bell family. They heard noises at night. Something knocked on their door. They heard a strange voice. They also heard scratching sounds. Their house sometimes shook.

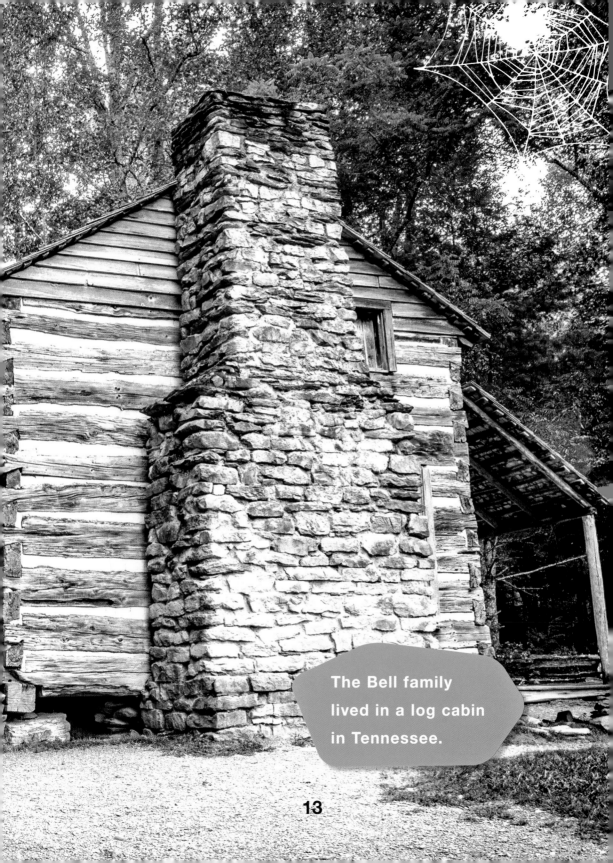

The Bell family lived in a log cabin in Tennessee.

It is said that the Bell Witch came into the Bells' house one night. The Bells were sleeping. The Bell Witch pulled the blankets off them. It attacked John's daughter. It pulled her hair. It slapped her.

BELL WITCH CAVE

The Bell family's farm was near the town of Adams, Tennessee. There is a cave nearby. Some people think the Bell Witch lives there.

John died in 1820. A bottle of poison was near his body. Some people think the Bell Witch killed him.

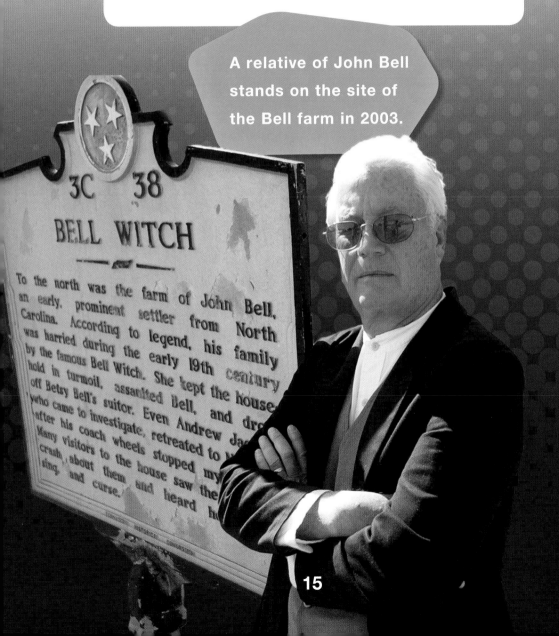

A relative of John Bell stands on the site of the Bell farm in 2003.

CHAPTER 3

THE GHOSTS OF the Stanley Hotel

Would you dare spend a night at the Stanley Hotel? Many people think this hotel is **haunted**. Some guests have seen ghosts. Some say there's a ghost in the **lobby**. They think it's Freelan Oscar Stanley's ghost.

Stanley **founded** the hotel in 1909. People report that his ghost wears a hat. They say he smiles at guests. People say his wife also haunts the hotel. Her name was Flora. There is a piano in the ballroom. Guests have heard piano music at night. They think it is Flora's ghost playing the music.

The Stanley Hotel is in Estes Park, Colorado.

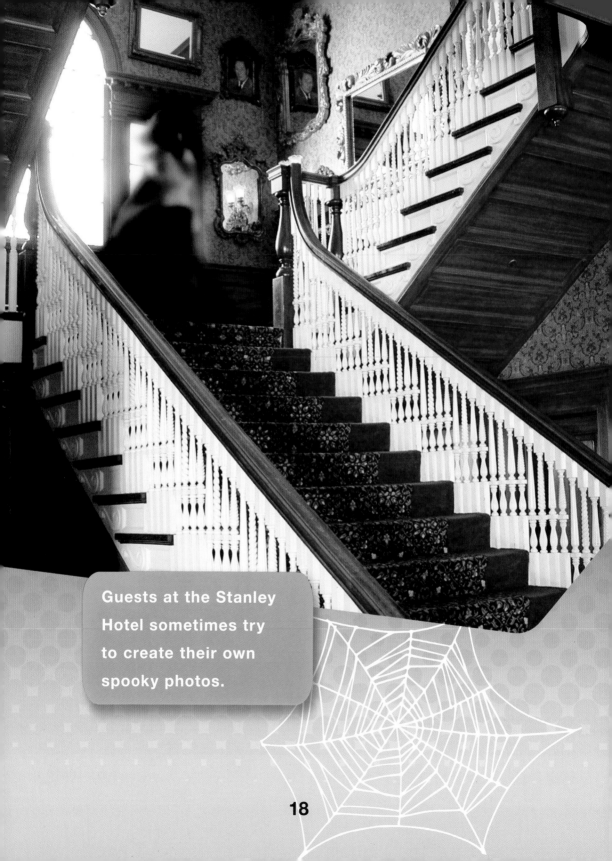

Guests at the Stanley Hotel sometimes try to create their own spooky photos.

In 2017 a guest took a photo. The photo showed a staircase inside the hotel. A white figure stood on the stairs. It looked like a ghost. Experts couldn't tell what the image was. But they say the photo was not **altered**.

THE SHINING

Author Stephen King stayed at the Stanley Hotel. He wrote a story based on his experience. The story is called *The Shining*.

CHAPTER 4

THE MAN in Grey

The Theatre Royal is a very old theater. It was first built in 1788. Some people think it's haunted. They say the ghosts of actors haunt the theater. People have heard sounds when no one is around. Some have heard doors slam.

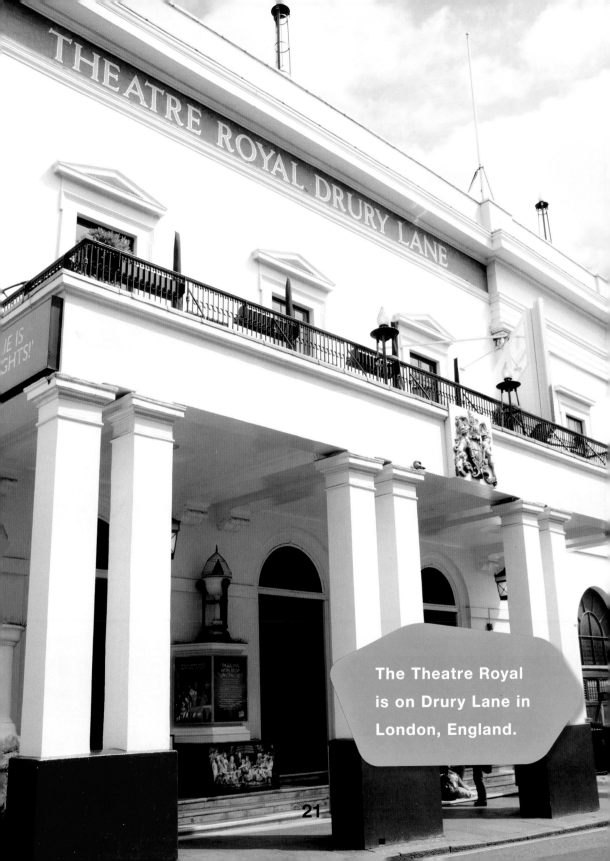

The Theatre Royal is on Drury Lane in London, England.

One ghost at the theater is the Man in Grey. Some call him the Drury Lane Ghost. He wears a long grey cloak. He stands with a sword. He travels through the theater's walls.

GHOST SIGHTINGS

Actors still perform at the Theatre Royal today. Some see the Man in Grey before they perform. They think this is good luck.

The Theatre Royal can fit more than 2,000 people.

CHAPTER 5

MARIE
Laveau

Marie Laveau lived in New Orleans, Louisiana. She lived in the 1800s. She was called the **Voodoo** Queen. She practiced voodoo. Voodoo is a religion. It says that people live in two worlds.

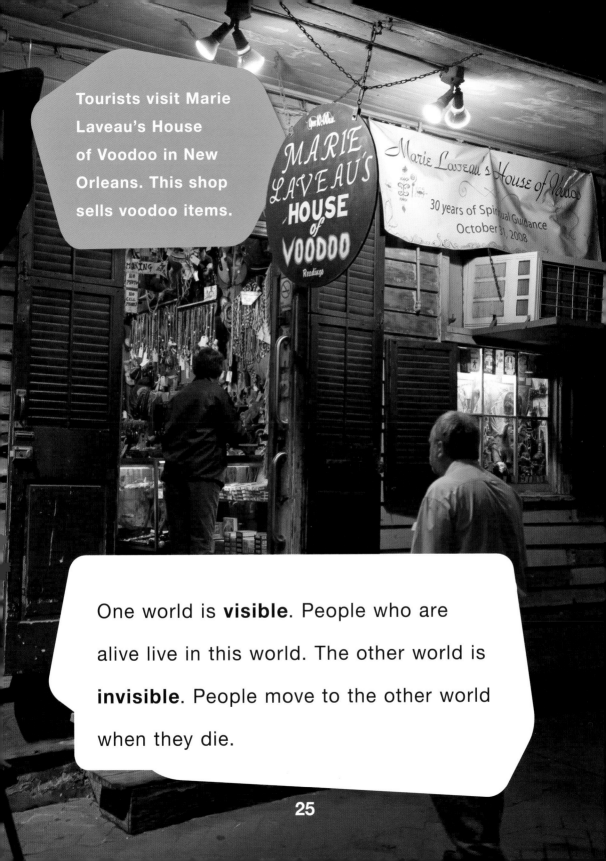

Tourists visit Marie Laveau's House of Voodoo in New Orleans. This shop sells voodoo items.

One world is **visible**. People who are alive live in this world. The other world is **invisible**. People move to the other world when they die.

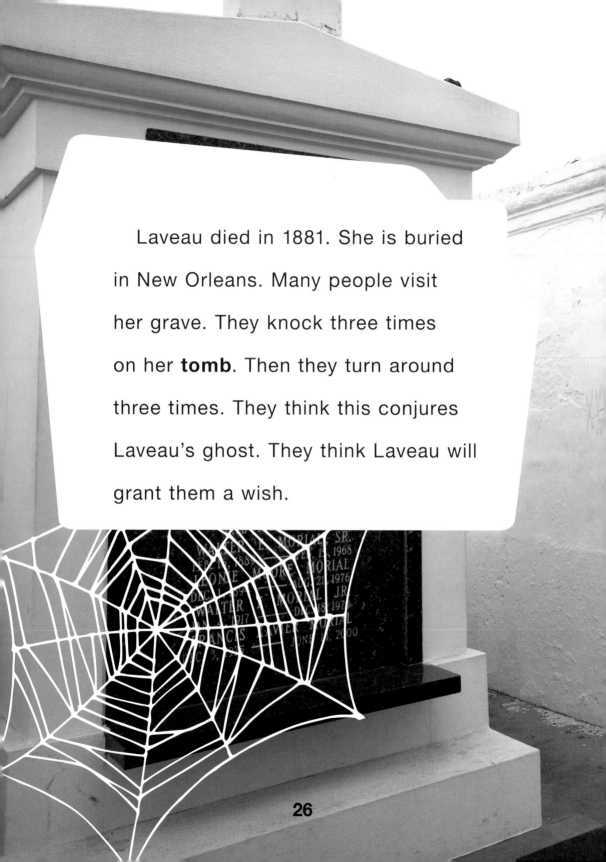

Laveau died in 1881. She is buried in New Orleans. Many people visit her grave. They knock three times on her **tomb**. Then they turn around three times. They think this conjures Laveau's ghost. They think Laveau will grant them a wish.

Laveau's tomb is in Saint Louis Cemetery in New Orleans.

GLOSSARY

altered
changed partly but not completely

conjure
to call a ghost or spirit

founded
to have established a business

haunted
having mysterious events happen often, possibly due to visits from ghosts

invisible
unable to be seen

lobby
an entryway

tomb
a burial chamber

visible
able to be seen

voodoo
a religion that started in Africa

witch
a person who is said to practice magic

TRIVIA

1. Some people think the Bloody Mary ghost is Mary Worth. Worth was said to be a witch. People say she kidnapped runaway slaves.

2. Stanley Hotel guests have heard many strange things. Some have heard footsteps in the halls. But when they look, no one is there. Some think the sounds come from the ghosts of children.

3. Two actors were at the Theatre Royal one night. They were preparing for a play. There was a TV in their room. The channel changed. But neither of the actors had touched it. They believe a ghost had changed the channel.

ACTIVITY

Choose your favorite ghost story from this book. Go online or visit a library to do more research. Record a short video about what you learned. You can do this with a smartphone or video camera. What new information did you learn about the ghost?

FURTHER RESOURCES

To discover more creepy ghost stories, check out these resources:

CBC Kids: Monster 101: All About Ghosts
http://www.cbc.ca/kidscbc2/the-feed/monsters-101-all-about-ghosts

The History Channel: History of Ghost Stories
http://www.history.com/topics/halloween/historical-ghost-stories

Raij, Emily. *The Most Haunted Places in the United States*. North Mankato, Minn.: Capstone Press, 2016.

Want to learn more about some of the ghosts in this book? Explore these resources:

Bougie, Matt. *The Bell Witch*. New York: Cavendish Square, 2017.

Loh-Hagan, Virginia. *Bloody Mary*. Ann Arbor, Mich.: Cherry Lake, 2018.

INDEX